# Theological Graffiti

Writings on the Wall of Belief

A. Deacon

**VANTAGE** Press
New York

FIRST EDITION

Published by Vantage Press, Inc.
419 Park Ave. South, New York, NY 10016

Manufactured in the United States of America
ISBN: 978-0-533-16339-7

Library of Congress Catalog Card No: 2010900542

0 9 8 7 6 5 4 3 2 1

# **Contents**

# Acknowledgments

My thanks to Hans Kung, Karen Armstrong, Raymond Brown, Michael Shermer, et al., whose writings have liberated my heart and mind from irrational dogma, and opened my soul to the "truth" associated with Christianity's journey through time.

# Introduction

I am not a religious scholar and make no claim to great intellectual insight or piety, nor is this work a comprehensive study of religion. If in fact, I was gifted with these traits, I would more eloquently seek to use these gifts to liberate Christianity from the burden of primitive forms of illogical belief. I would labor to accomplish this by seeking the establishment of a practice of religious worship whose theology was focused on the attributes of hope and love, and devoid of practices built upon a foundation of the supernatural.

It is not my intent to discredit anyone's religious belief. In fact, I believe that humanity needs its religious-based faiths, perhaps to a greater degree, than at any time in our historic journey through time. As for Christianity, what I do seek is to promote an understanding of our faith's tradition that is compatible with twenty-first-century reality. A faith interpretation grounded in reality is far less vulnerable to attack by nonbelievers, or new archeological discoveries that could discredit dogmatic tenets of faith.

Since I personally subscribe to reality-based faith interpretations, it matters not to me if tomorrow Jesus' bodily remains were found and identified by competent scientists. Why? ... because Jesus, the man and his teachings, are what is important to me. He, and his ministry, mirrored those attributes and wisdom that we attribute to our Creator. The truth of the man, the wisdom tradition he emerged from, and what he revealed to us is what really counts.

Why I have chosen to do this is based on my love for my Catholic Christian faith. As an ordained deacon within this faith's tradition, I want it to grow in relevance in the centuries to follow, rather than shrink to a state of irrelevance. My concern, as it relates to the threat of irrelevance, is based on my belief that as humanity's understanding of reality becomes based more on scientific method, humanity will increasingly reject faith explanations confined to the literal interpretations of events that are portrayed as supernatural. Recent polls taken to measure the nature of people's religious beliefs corroborate my concern, in that they indicate that the number of our citizens who profess no belief in God is growing as a percentage of the total population (Pew Forum on Religion and Public Life).

Could it be that in the daily struggles of life, where there is a continuing need to solve problems in the here-and-now, religious beliefs cloaked in supernatural myth can no longer compete with scientific methods?

It is my belief that when the writers of Christian Scripture took up the pen to describe Jesus of Nazareth and the nature and impact of his ministry, they did so within the context of Hebrew Scripture. This makes sense, because Jesus and his ministry were a direct product of his Jewish faith's tradition. By so framing him and his ministry within this context, the gospel writers made him, and his ministry understandable to their Jewish readers. Jewish readers, you might ask? Yes, for Jewish readers were the primary audience of their time. For, we must remember, Jesus, his apostles, Paul, and three of the four of the gospel writers, were not only Jews, but very observant Jews. Of the gospel writers, only Luke is believed to have been a non-Palestinian Gentile[1] So when the gospel writers sought to define the ministry and person of Jesus, and what followed, they did so not within the context of a modern historical interpretation, but through the theological lens of how they viewed the world. The Jesus they wrote of was described and defined within the framework of his, and their, Jewish faith. A tradition that employed allegory as a tool to capture the attention of readers, and enable them to gain an understanding of the meaning and value of what was being described to them.

Scientific methods are not the enemy of Christianity. In fact, they can be the instrument by which we can gain a better understanding of how and why our Christian faith has been gifted to us by those who preceded us. To employ a well-known analogy, how many of us, as children, believed in the myth of Santa Claus? In my case, I remember it as a wonderful mystery associated with many joyful Christmas mornings. How much more wonderful was it when we eventually learned the reality behind the myth of Santa Claus, and that it was our loving parents who were in fact responsible for the joy and wonder we experienced. So, as in the case of the myth of Santa Claus, perhaps we can experience the same level of joy by reexamining the myths associated with our faith's traditions. The allegorical portrayals within Hebrew and Christian Scriptures could well hide deeper levels of truth and joyfulness than any literal interpretation of either.

The ideas expressed in this text have all been thought of and written about by others far more talented than me. Nothing that hasn't been thought of before is presented here. I seek no credit for the labors of others. Rather, my purpose is to draw you further into the thoughtful search for interpretations of your faith beliefs that are in harmony with the reality of everyday experience. It just doesn't make any sense to me for us to rely on the fruits of scientific methods (medicine, chemistry, transportation, physics, communications, space exploration, etc.) in our daily lives, and then reject their explanations as to our origin, or relationship to our universe.

As for my identity, I seek anonymity. Why, may you ask? My answer is, because even though I am a person of no significance, I want the ideas that I profess to be the center of discussion, rather than having it be on me personally as a heretical dissenting cleric. As an ordained minister (a permanent deacon), I am expected, in my public utterances, to conform to the teachings of my church's authority. So on a day-to-day basis, I keep my modernist thoughts to myself, and focus on helping others in their daily struggles. In fact my identity is not really relevant to what is presented within this text.

What is important to me is that the thoughts expressed within this text will prompt further thoughtful inquiries by you, the reader.

However, to allow you, the reader, to evaluate how my particular life experiences may have given rise to any potential bias, or particular orientation on my part, I describe myself as follows:

A male born into a working class family within the United States of America and of European ancestry;

A practicing Catholic since early childhood, including three years of elementary-school education in parochial schools;

Military service (27 years) in an active and reserve status;

Married (48 years) with two adult children;

Primary career (more than 33 years) in law enforcement within a large urban metropolitan area;

University degrees at the undergraduate and graduate levels within the disciplines of behavioral and political science;

Ordained as a permanent deacon within the Catholic Church.

I do admit to an existential bias, in that as a police officer, the day-to day reality I experienced on the streets of the city that I served left its indelible mark on my soul. My survival required submission to this reality. The citizens I served demanded actions that met their needs in the here-and-now. As a consequence, over the years, my religious beliefs were put to the test. Especially those dogmatic beliefs that failed to adequately explain how bad things could happen to the innocent. Specifically, as in one case, as to how a loving God, who was active in the world, could allow the brutal molestation and murder of a four-year-old innocent. Enough said, you can judge for yourself.

# Theological Graffiti

# 1

# The Beginning of Physical Reality

"It is as easy to believe in God, as it is to believe in 'Black Holes' (Dark Matter)."

If you, the reader, are having difficulty reconciling your faith's religious beliefs relating to the origin of our universe with twenty-first century scientific explanations, don't blame the early authors of Hebrew Scripture. The blame lies with the religious teachers of our time for their unwillingness to admit to the allegorical nature of scriptural writings describing creation.

Several different sources, or literary traditions (known as the Yahwist [J], the Elohis [E], and the Priestly [P]), contributed to the recounting of the origin of the world found in Genesis.[2] Each chronicled God's creative works in theological, not scientific, terms. They had no other choice but to employ that knowledge of the world that they possessed at that moment in time. Since they viewed their world through the lens of their theological beliefs, they were limited primarily to the use of folktales and mythology to communicate to their faithful. As a consequence, what we read in Genesis today is understood by scholars to have been signifi-cantly influenced by Canaanite and Babylonian myth traditions. Considering that in the sixth century B.C.E. the elite of Israelite society spent at least fifty years in Babylonian captivity, it is not hard to understand the 'how and why' these foreign faith tradi-tions had considerable influence on the development of Jewish theology. Again, not their fault, they only knew what they knew at that moment in time, so just remember, the same applies to us.

Just because these priestly writers lacked the resources of modern science to accurately describe the astrological processes associated with the creation of our physical universe this does not diminish the value of their inspired writings. For it was their purpose to proclaim the why of creation, not the how of creation. In this regard, their genius has withstood the test of time.

The "P" priestly tradition is classically described as a creation of the exilic or postexilic period (sixth or fifth century B.C.E.). It stressed Israelite ritual and religious observance. It proclaimed to their faithful that Yahweh had divine control over worldly events that transcended any human power. Humankind was described as having been created in their creator's image, and that they, as Yahweh's people, were obligated to behave as Yahweh would behave. This behavioral expectation became the basis of the Jews' convential relationship with their god.[3]

The "J" priestly tradition is thought to have originated in Jerusalem and is dated to the ninth or tenth century B.C.E. Its characteristics include the frequent use of anthropomorphism in depictions of Yahweh. It emphasized the nature of humankind's inclination to sin, the relationship of punishment to sinful acts, and the redemptive hope that despite their failures, Yahweh would always regard them as his chosen people.[4]

The "E" priestly tradition had its source in the northern kingdom (930–722 B.C.E.) and harbored an anti-Jerusalem bias. Its teachings emphasized covenant over kingship. At some point during the seventh century B.C.E., conquest of the northern kingdom by the Assyrians, the Elohist priestly tradition was carried south to Judah by refugees fleeing the Assyrian onslaught and was incorporated into the two surviving priestly traditions.[5]

We of the twenty-first century are greatly privileged and blessed to have the resources of both science and religion to answer our questions related to the how and why of our existence.

Our lives, compared to those who preceded us, have been materially transformed through the application of scientific methods to explain the reality in which we live. However, answering the question of how is not enough in and of itself. Our human nature also demands that we know the why of our existence. For this, science can be of little help. This knowledge can best be acquired by examining the lessons learned over the centuries by those who preceded us. In this, we are also fortunate, in that we have not only the resources of scientific methods to enable us to discern how we came to be, but also the wisdom of our ancestors, revealed in the Sacred Scripture, to explain the why.

As of this juncture in time, it is the scientific consensus that we live within an expanding universe. This is what is considered the "Standard Model" hypothesis, which is commonly labeled the "Primeval Atom" or "Big Bang" theory. Interestingly, this hypothesis was formulated by a Catholic theologian/astrophysicist named Abbe Georges Lemaitre (1894–1966).[6]

Recent astrological observations have confirmed Lemaitre's theory, through findings that indicate that our universe is expanding at an ever increasing rate. These observations support the hypothesis that in the beginning all the energy and matter comprising our universe was compressed into an unimaginably tiny and hot fireball of the smallest dimensions and the greatest density and temperature. At some point, up to thirteen to fifteen billion years ago, this hot fireball exploded, and hence the term the "Big Bang."[7] A big bang that could conceivably have been the product of divine design. Why not—there is no proof that it wasn't.

While science can help us to understand what happened after the "Big Bang," it has not been able give us a clue as to the origin of the matter that became the source of our universe. This information may always be beyond our grasp, because the answer to that question may lie beyond our physical universe, to which we in life are confined. For us, knowledge is acquired through observation and our ability to relate our findings to experience.

3

This gives us a frame of reference, by which to facilitate an understanding of what we have observed. That which is beyond our ability to observe, and relate to experience, is beyond our ability to know. The closest we can get to answering questions relating to that which lies beyond the range of our senses, is to deductively discern the presence of that reality by the effect of its influence on the observable. Since the presence of "dark matter," astronomers tell us, can be deductively discerned by its influence on the orbits of visible stars, could not humankind's faith experiences through time be used in the same manner to deductively discern the presence of God's spirit within us?

As a consequence of our inability to discern what lies beyond our universe, neither science nor religion can empirically prove the existence or absence of a divine Creator. Belief, or non-belief, in a divine Creator is analogous to a belief that a glass of water is half full, or half empty. We have to decide this question on the basis of faith. Fortunately, for the religious of the world, we have been gifted with a faithful optimism—based on the experiences of those who preceded us through the millennia of time—to believe that the glass is half full.

However, our understanding of the tenets of our faith need not be the same as those from earlier times. As in nature, all things evolve and adapt in accordance with experience and the forces of reality. It is the same with religious beliefs, as what does not adapt, dies. In accordance with this reality, the Catholic Church has long recognized tradition as a guiding force in the development of its theology. However, as the history of the church indicates, it often takes hundreds of years for the church to recognize and assimilate new concepts of understanding. The Church's reaction to Copernicus' findings, relating to our solar system, is a case in point. In his time his discoveries were considered heretical, while we in our time consider his observations an obvious reality. Both science and religious beliefs associated with the creation of our universe both acknowledge that there was a beginning to our physical reality. Whatever the source, the reality that you and I live in is also acknowledged by science to be governed by certain forces, which we call laws (quantum, Newtonian, biological, et al.). It can also be inferred that these governing forces were set, or became operative, at the moment of the birth of our universe in varying degrees up to the present. For those of us who believe that God set this process in motion, then it could also be logically deduced that these governing forces could be attributes of that God's very nature.

If the physical forces cited (quantum, Newtonian, biological, et al.) do reflect attributes of our Creator's nature and are the governing forces that shape reality within our universe, then what part does the supernatural play in this scheme of things? In my opinion, the supernatural plays no part in the natural scheme of things. By definition, a supernatural event is an event that allegedly occurs in contravention to those natural laws that govern physical reality. So, if we as religious believers attribute the laws that govern the reality of our universe to the very nature of our Creator/God, then it could be deduced that any belief in the supernatural would be inconsistent with a belief in that same God.

If not from God, then from what source does the realm of the supernatural spring? I say from the mind of humankind. It should be classified in terms of what we now categorize as "virtual reality." It is a nonmaterial human construct whose purpose is to explain the inexplicable, sometimes in allegorical terms. It is the stuff of folktales and must be recognized for what it is ... a human construct. Confusing the supernatural with reality is to lose the prospective of the real world that we live in. Preoccupation with the supernatural, in my opinion, is in fact dangerous, as it distorts understandings related to the challenges we face in the real world. The survival of every social institution is dependent upon its ability to accurately interpret the challenges that confront it in the real world, to develop relevant coping strategies, and communicate these strategies to its members in a timely manner. Any failure to accomplish this dooms the institution/belief system to oblivion. Remember, we, the religious faithful, need not be afraid of what science reveals to us. Instead, we should strive to look for the beauty in its revelations related to the how. For these revelations can serve to provide us with a new frame of reference by which we can come to a new understanding of the true complexity and majesty of the why.

# 2

# Evolution

**"Our religious faith teaches us why we were created by a loving God, while science describes how it was done."**

Based on my life experiences and religious studies, I have reached the conclusion that our Creator directly influences our physical reality in two fundamental ways. First, if we accept the belief that God is the source of our reality and that those laws that govern our universe are a reflection of our Creator's very nature, then it should follow that our universe's birth and evolution were and are currently dependent upon God. In my mind, the forces I describe as attributes of God are those same physical laws acknowledged by science as the forces that govern our reality. However, I am not suggesting an active conscious God-driven relationship between these forces and our physical world. It does not make sense to me to believe that God consciously controls what happens in the universe.

Following some natural disaster, such as an earthquake, tornados, a flood, etc., I have often heard these events referred to as "acts of God." As if, in this vast universe, our loving God doesn't have anything better to do than occasionally arrange for us to suffer the consequences of some natural calamity. Is it not time that we humans take responsibility for the consequences of our own actions, like building a house in a flood plain, close to an earthquake fault, or in tornado alleys? The truth of the matter is that it is not God that places some of us in harm's way. We find ourselves the victims of these phenomena as the result of actions initiated by either ourselves, or someone else.

Regarding God's attributes as having an influence on our physical world, I would categorize this interaction as autonomic in nature. In the same way our bodily functions are unconsciously regulated by our autonomic nervous system, so could God's presence influence our reality in the same manner. While it may be comforting to believe that these events have a source and purpose, which we attribute to a divine action, labeling them as "acts of God," such a rationalization is inconsistent with a belief in a God who cares for our welfare. In my opinion, events that we categorize as disasters are merely the product of the forces that shape the world in which we live. We are like fleas on an elephant, we go where the elephant goes and share the fate of the beast on which we dwell. The fact that, like fleas, we find ourselves in a particular location that exposes us to a natural disaster is just a consequence of living on a planet that is still evolving. If it didn't have these characteristics, it would not be suitable for habitation by living life forms. The risk associated with living on a planet capable of supporting life is the price we pay for enjoying the privilege of living.

The second way I see God's influence in our world lies within the realm of human activity. We, like all other things in our world, have been shaped by those laws that reflect God's nature. Our evolutionary journey has brought us to a very unique state of being. We, unlike any other creature on this planet, have been gifted with the facility of abstract thought. While other life forms are governed by instinct, we have the capability to overrule instinctual behaviors through the use of our intellect—an intellect which allows us to make conscious "free-will" decisions. Decisions that can override our own selfish interests to the benefit of others. We have the unique capacity of consciousness that enables us to gauge how our actions might negatively, or positively, impact others. We describe this capability as having a "conscience." These are qualities that the religious faithful say mirror the qualities of our Creator. In this regard, we are truly unique among all other creatures.

I see no conflict between Darwin's observations and his thesis relating to the origins of the world's various species, including Homo sapiens, and my religious beliefs. It is my understanding that Darwin's essential thesis relates to his understanding that all life on earth has evolved over time, under the influence of those natural laws that govern our world. My reaction to his observations, is, but of course. How could life not be shaped by those laws that govern our world? Also, the evolutionary process in which we find ourselves a part of is not static. It is continuous and dynamic. As you read these words, you, the reader, and I, are actually evolving from what we were, to something that we will become. Nothing alive is exempt from the forces that shape our reality, for what does not yield to its influence, invites extinction.

A religious person might ask, "But how could this be, if we believe that all life was created by God?" My response to that question would be to point out that if the laws that govern our world are attributes of the very nature of God, then Darwin's thesis is the vehicle for gaining an understanding of how God acts in the world. Remember, Darwin was seeking to describe an observable reality, while the authors of Genesis sought to chronicle that all things had their source in God. Each labored with the tools of his time, and each reached conclusions that were consistent with his particular understanding of reality. Just remember, you and I only know what we know up to this very moment in time. Hopefully, tomorrow both of us will know more than we do at this moment in time. A thousand years from now, if we haven't destroyed the habitability of this planet, humanity's level of knowledge should be light-years ahead of where we are now.

In his book, *Life's Solution: Inevitable Humans in a Lonely Universe,* Conway Morris, a professor of evolutionary paleobiology, challenges conventional scientific skepticism associated with the belief that evolution has an overall design, and perhaps even a purpose. While skeptics see evolution as an effectively random process where any outcome is possible, Dr. Morris finds evidence that points in the opposite direction. His findings strongly point to findings that the evolutionary process has an uncanny knack of navigating to precise solutions. He cites evidence which demonstrates that following the disappearance of some life forms on earth, following catastrophic events, the new life forms that emerged showed traits that indicate that the evolutionary process repeatedly returns to the same solutions, which suggests evolutionary convergence. Specific examples of convergence are seen especially in the acquisition of "camera-eyes" in widely diverse life forms such as the octopus and humans.[8]

The apparent randomness of the results of evolutionary processes suggests to some scientists that there is no apparent design or purpose to our reality. Randomness is equated with chaos, in that there is no way to predict the outcome of its processes. Thus the random and chaotic nature of these processes is cited by non-religious persons as proof that our origins could not have their source in a divine Creator.

I have a different view regarding the apparent randomness, or chaotic nature, of the evolutionary processes at all levels, especially at the quantum level. While acknowledging the unpredictability of the evolutionary process, I do not view this characteristic of randomness as evidence that our reality has no purpose or design. Where others see chaos, I see perfection. To me the chaotic nature of evolution confirms in my mind the adage that "God's ways are not man's way." I base my belief on my understanding that any process that does exhibit predictability does so as a result of having attributes which constrain its output. Such a process's output is constrained by the very boundaries that any defined structure must have in order to ensure output predictability. Therefore, predictability can only be achieved at the cost of the exclusion of the infinite range of possibilities. This exclusion of the infinite range of possibilities suggests to me that our universe could never have evolved to its current level of complexity had evolution been dependent upon a structured system whose output was predictable. So, I would agree that the reality in which we live is the product of an indefinable process.

In my mind, such an unstructured evolutionary system whose output is described as unpredictable, because its attributes can best be described as random, or chaotic, should be recognized as the only system capable of ensuring that no range of possibilities is excluded from its processes. Having no defined structure precludes it from excluding any range of the infinite from its machinations. By its openness to every possible combination of processes, it should be viewed as the perfect system, one worthy of being identified as an attribute of a divine Creator.

# 3

# What Distinguishes Us from Other Life Forms?

**"We have the capacity to turn our dreams into reality."**

As for our origin, both Hebrew Scripture (Genesis, chapter 2, verse 7) and science describe us as springing forth from the soil of the planet earth.[9] No conflict here. We are what we are, a species of a mammalian primate that has evolved through several million years of time, to our present form of Homo sapiens. A creature more like our fellow creatures than we are different. Since the writers of Genesis lacked the resources of scientific methods to describe how we evolved to our current state of being, they used the only tool or frame of reference at their disposal—namely, their theologically mythological tradition—to describe why God gifted us with his attributes. Again, these writers of antiquity were not as interested in describing the how their god accomplished this, as they were in revealing the why our god did this. As I stated previously, in our present time, we currently have resources available to us that our ancestors didn't have thousands of years ago. Thanks to scientific methods, we now have the advantage of understanding both how and why a slight chromosomal difference distinguishes us from all other life forms on this planet.

While I subscribe to a science-based explanation of our origin, some religious persons, typically called fundamentalists, still cling to the theological/mythological model portrayed in Genesis. These fundamentalists subscribe to a literal interpretation of the Genesis creation story, ignoring its allegorical qualities. Those fundamentalists that I have encountered through the years who espouse this literalist orientation don't seem to value what the scientific method has revealed to us relating to the origin of our reality. They also resist suggestions that they should be open to the opportunity to look beyond mythological explanations relating to our origins and test the validity of their literal interpretations of the scripture. Instead they formulate alternative supernatural theories relating to our origins under the label of creationism, etc. Unfortunately, these alterative theories are built on foundations of myth, and are vulnerable to critical analysis.

With the exception of some religious sects who reject twenty-first-century reality in an attempt to live out their lives in a manner consistent with an eighteenth century agrarian pseudo reality, I find the practice of this antiscientific orientation hypocritical. The hypocrisy associated with fundamentalism is revealed through observations that while these adherents reject science's explanations relating to our origins, they eagerly make use of the benefits science provides them in their daily lives. As folklore tells us: "You can't have your cake and eat it too!" To believe that you can is the height of hypocrisy. To truly be faithful to this antiscientific orientation, and avoid being labeled as a hypocrite, may I suggest that adherents to fundamentalism divest themselves of all the benefits that scientific method has bestowed upon them. Yes, I am suggesting that if fundamentalists want to maintain any sense of credibility, they must divest themselves of their motor vehicles, medical/dental care, use of modern mass transportation systems, computers, television, firearms, and anything else that is a product of a scientific method.

The reality that we are faced with is that we humans evolved over eons of time to become what we are. This doesn't mean that God didn't have a hand in this process. It does suggest that the process of our creation was a lot more complex than that which is portrayed in a literal interpretation of Genesis. Just as in the reality of the Christmas celebration story, the revealed truth of our origins can be much more beautifully complex than the mythical representation.

Three and a half billion years ago complex life forms appeared on earth. Homo-erectus appeared one and a half billion years ago, while Homo sapiens made their appearance a mere two hundred thousand years ago. Even prior to the appearance of Homo sapiens, at about two and a half million years ago, the pre-ancestors of our species were making tools, and had mastered the use of fire. This strongly suggests that these pre-species of Homo sapiens were even forming into groups, which would further infer that they had developed some form of communication to facilitate survival strategies associated with the acquisition of food, shelter, etc. Michael Shermer, in his book *The Science of Good & Evil: Why People Cheat, Gossip, Care, Share, and Follow the Golden Rule,* describes this evolutionary process of how our uniquely human qualities evolved far more eloquently, and in greater detail, than I could ever describe. For anyone who wants to gain an understanding of the specifics of this process, I recommend that you read his book.

In summary, Shermer's research indicates that our unique facility of human consciousness was acquired over time through the necessity of our ancestors' need to participate in cooperative efforts associated with group survival. The dynamics associated with group social interactions over the eons of time stimulated the development of the human brain, giving it the capability of consciousness. The attribute of consciousness became the necessary precursor for the development of speech. Speech then facilitated the further development of even more complex social interactions, which in turn led to further development of the human brain. We Homo sapiens are the current product of this continuing evolutionary process, the end result of which, will be constrained only by the limits of our imagination.

One can only speculate as to the point, within the eons of evolutionary time, when our ancestors became fully human and began to mirror those attributes we attribute to our God. I certainly don't know when this occurred. Within the span of my lifetime, anthropologists have discovered primitive peoples deep in isolated rainforests, who had no previous contact with outsiders. Up to the time of their discovery, they lived as our ancient stone-age ancestors did. Although they lived very primitive lives and had no concept of our beliefs and value systems, can we say that they were any less human than us? I doubt it. Perhaps this best describes how we should judge the spiritual potentiality of those who preceded us. What is known to us presently is that we as humans stand distinct from all other life forms on this planet by virtue of our ability to conceptualize that which did not exist up to this particular moment in time. Perhaps, this unique attribute of creativity is empowered by that part of us which we call the soul, which reflects God's spirit within us.

# 4

# Original Sin

**"The collision between our egocentric nature and the constraints of conscience is the price we pay for being human."**

The Catechism of the Catholic Church defines "original sin" as: "The sin by which the first human beings disobeyed the commandment of God, choosing to follow their own will rather than God's will. As a consequence they lost the grace of original holiness, and became subject to the law of death; sin became universally present in the world. Besides the personal sin of Adam and Eve, original sin describes the fallen state of human nature which affects every person born into the world, and from which Christ, the 'new Adam,' came to redeem us."[10]

As evolving mammals, we humans are caught between two competing realities. On the one hand, we are primevally "hardwired" to seek survival through acts, which can best be classified as egocentric. However, conversely, in order to achieve our goals, we must restrain our egocentric tendencies and employ behavioral strategies that allow us to secure the cooperation of others. This conflict arises from the fact that, while we are a predatory entity, prone to exhibit behavior which seeks domination over others, evolution has brought us to a point in time where our survival is largely dependent upon the supportive actions of others. A fact that requires us, if we are to be successful in any endeavor, to strike a balance between these two behavioral extremes.

Each of us matures from childhood to adulthood within the context of a community of others. This community is operative at various levels ranging from the nuclear family to the extended family, the neighborhood, tribe, clan, religious affiliation, township, nation state, etc. At each level we are exposed to a process of socialization that has as its purpose the subordination of our selfish inclinations for the benefit of the community in which we live.

Failure to observe the constraints imposed by a social group will result in some form of sanction. Group sanctions can range from informal acts of disapproval or restraint, to formal sanctions under the color of law. When the individual successfully learns to function effectively within the group for his/her benefit and the group's benefit, we consider the individual successfully socialized. When attempts at socialization fail to restrict the individual's actions that are at variance with the community's interests, the individual can expect the larger group to react in a manner that seeks to ameliorate the egocentric behavior. Societies label those whom they fail to socialize and seek to sanction as sinners, misfits, psychopaths, or criminals.

Religious groups have long understood our predisposition to seek self-gratification through egocentric acts, and the need to lessen the negative aspects of this behavior on the larger community. This predisposition has been labeled as the inclination to sin, with sin representing the most egregious forms of egocentric behavior. The Sacrament of Baptism has long been recognized as the instrument by which a person could be freed from this inclination and integrated into the larger community. Recognition of this need for integration underscores the importance of striking a balance between the often competing interests of the individual and those of the community. Successful communities strike this balance by encouraging egocentricity, which, while satisfying individual needs, supports the larger community's goals. Where widespread imbalances between individual and group needs occur, the survival of both is at risk.

Within the United States, we are currently witnessing evidence of this imbalance within several religious sects. This imbalance is arising from conflict associated with a clash between various religious institutions' attempts to regulate behavior, and individual efforts to expand the boundaries of self-expression. What is viewed as a sin by one group, is being contested by others. Only time will tell who is a sinner, and who isn't.

In my opinion (as exemplified by Adam and Eve's behavior) what the Christian Church labels as "original sin" is in reality humanity's predisposition to antisocial egocentric behavior. Only specifically defined antisocial acts, not predispositions, should be categorized as a sin. Sin, by my understanding, can only arise from the commission of an act by a mentally competent individual, who, through the exercise of free will, knowingly violates a tenet of a religious belief tradition. As such, no person or generation can pass their sins to a succeeding generation, as only the individual who committed the act can be held accountable. However, we can pass on, from one generation to another, our human predispositions and vulnerabilities to sinful behavior. The transmission of these very human traits from one generation to another is the price we pay for the privilege of birth into an imperfect universe.

# 5

# The Evolution of Ethical Behavior

**"Mortality springs forth from our God given nature."**

In Genesis, chapter 2, verses 15–17, sacred scripture presents us with an allegorical lesson related to the source of behavioral expectations, and the sanctions associated with nonadherence. It reads: "The Lord God then took the man and settled him in the Garden of Eden, to cultivate and care for it. The Lord God gave this order: You are free to eat from any of the trees of the garden, except the tree of knowledge of good and bad. From that tree you shall not eat; the moment you eat from it you are surely doomed to die."[11]

Well, we all know what happened there. Adam and Eve, despite the clearly defined expectation and sanction, ate the forbidden fruit upon being encouraged to do so. They did this so that they might become like the gods, and gain the knowledge of what is good and what is bad. The moral lesson being that, while this act of disobedience did grant them knowledge of right and wrong, it did so at the cost of being banished from the idyllic garden created to meet all their needs. In short, they lost more than they gained. How many of us, or others known to us, have suffered similar fates as the result of violating a societal norm, or law?

Where do these societal expectations (informal/legal) come from? Do they have their source in God, as claimed in Genesis, or do they have their origin elsewhere? Several additional instances of behavioral norm settings are described in sacred scripture, besides the one previously cited. These norms are summarized in the covenant with Abram, in Noah, in the covenant at Mount Sinai, in Deuteronomy, and the Christian covenant. Does the fact that our religious faith traditions devote considerable emphasis to defining, promoting and enforcing specific behavioral expectations mean that they are God-driven and absolute? Or, do they have a more earthly ancient source, and only apply to specific situations?

Even if our religious traditions are correct as to the God-driven nature of ethical norms, one thing is clear from reading sacred scripture: they evolved over time. It doesn't take a rocket scientist to note that even in scripture, the behavioral norms that govern our lives are shown to have evolved over the millennia of time from the simple to the complex. To this religion-based conclusion, even science can agree.

In his book, *"The Beginning of All Things, Science and Religion,* Catholic theologian Hans Kung states that even in primitive cultures, such as those found in Africa and Australia, with no writing, science, and technology, they had a civilization. Their thought was judged to be logical, plausible, and shaped by a passion for order, and by the classifying of things and relationships. In short, primitive though they may have been upon their discovery by Europeans, these primitive cultures possessed well-defined systems of normative expectations. By virtue of this fact, only their lack of technology separated them from those who discovered them. Both discoverer and discovered shared the central characteristic that made them both human, a system of ethical values rooted in "reciprocal altruism." Ethical values that encouraged:

a sense of mutuality;
a reverence for life;
rules for sexes living together;
and respect for parents and the care of children.

So despite the fact that up to their discovery, these primitive civilizations did not have the benefit of Judaic-Christian teachings, they nevertheless had, over the millennia of time, developed systems of ethical behavior which paralleled the ethical systems of those who had discovered them. So, the question is raised: How did they do this? Did God play a role in this—if so, how?

In his book, *The Science of Good and Evil: Why People Cheat, Gossip, Care, Share, and Follow the Golden Rule,* psychologist and science historian Michael Shermer reveals to his readers the how and why we humans made the leap from a social primate to a moral primate. Shermer, as a skeptic, does not see this process as God-driven, but rather a product of necessity. Necessity rooted in humankind's need to seek survival through the formation of social groups. However, despite his skepticism that this process could be God-driven, Shermer's study of this phenomenon has led him to believe that morality is deeply embedded in our being and behavior. [12] I find this statement very interesting, for it suggests to me that humankind's search for survival, within the context of social systems that value the rule of "reciprocal altruism" (the Golden Rule), springs from the very core of our human nature. A nature that, religion teaches us, mirrors the qualities of our Creator.

While behavior which can be labeled as "reciprocal altruism" is not unique to humans, as primates, bats and social insects also have been observed to engage in behavior of an altruistic nature, its practice by these other cited life forms is far less complex than the degree to which it manifests itself in human interactions. Typically, altruistic behavior observed in nonhuman life-form interactions is limited to behavior associated with communal food gathering and sharing, grooming, mutual defense, and care of offspring. As you can see, reciprocal altruism, even in its most basic forms, can be quickly seen for what it is, a very important survival mechanism. A mode of behavior driven by the necessity to survive, whose roots predate religion, and upon which the foundation of human morality is built—morality being defined as a set of behavioral rules governing members of a human social order. The right or wrong, good or evil, of an individual's act within a given social order is subject to the judgment of his or her peers. At this level, morality is unique to humans, as behavioral acts at this level require a conscious understanding of the nature of the act and its consequences. There can be no right or wrong, nor good or evil, without humanity's ability to know what the expectations of a particular social system are in which the individual finds himself, or herself. For an act of a human to be judged as good, or evil, there must have been a conscious decision to act in a particular manner, with the person knowing what the consequences associated with the act are. As you can see, this requires the facility of abstract thought. This is why nonhuman life forms, whose acts are governed by instinct, are incapable of committing an immoral act. In short, in the absence of the human capability of making a free-will decision, there can be no act deemed to be good or evil.

The bottom line regarding the origin of what we now call moral behavior (behavior within the context of rules defining right and wrong) is that it is a product of our evolution as a species. Again, my point is that we have evolved over the millennia of time, changing physically, growing mentally, and acquiring those traits that enable us to function within highly complex social systems. Social systems which have, by necessity, forced us to restrict our own egocentric impulses and act in ways that are compatible with the sentiments and needs of others. These sentiments and needs of others, Shermer says, become a form of moral behavioral control, with moral behavioral control being an essential component of hierarchical social orders, upon which their members are dependent for their survival. So, the price we paid for survival through the ages was the sublimation of individual ego fulfillment, which was inconsistent with the needs of the larger group. While individual sublimation of ego driven behavior for the larger group's benefit did not necessarily translate into a evolutionary advantage for the individual, it did translate into an evolutionary advantage for groups. This is because once our human ancestors formed into social groups as part of a survival strategy, evolutionary competition shifted from the individual level to the group level. Groups that were better able to focus individual member behavior toward the fulfillment of group goals gained a distinct evolutionary advantage over those groups that could not achieve unanimity.

Unanimity with any group is a product of shared values—values that have their origin in sentiments acquired over time during humanity's experiences in the real world. The greater the degree of unanimity within a group, the lower the incidence of conflict between individual members. Conflicts that do arise are far more likely to be settled amicably in groups where shared values are the norm, because both sides to an argument are more likely to submit to a higher authority's resolution of a dispute. This fact translates into less friction within the group, more respect for the group's leadership, which gives the group as a whole an evolutionary advantage over competing groups. So, to the degree that individuals within a social order value and practice what we call moral behavior, the rules defining right and wrong, the greater is the probability that the group will gain an evolutionary edge over competing groups unable to achieve an equal level of unanimity.

As for the source of humankind's need to seek group unanimity driven by recognized rules of moral conduct, I agree with Shermer when he says that it springs from our very nature. A nature that reflects those attributes inherited from that force from which all things within our universe have their source, and which we religious folks call God. While Shermer, a skeptic, would disagree as to morality having a God-driven source, he does attribute humankind's need for moral conduct to be deeply embedded within our being. In other words, despite his skepticism related to this trait being God-driven, his research and observations point to a belief that altruistic moral behavior is intrinsic to our very nature. While we may disagree as to its source, we can agree that the constraints of moral behavior are unique to humankind, and that their complexity has paralleled our maturation over the millennia of time.

Now you might ask, "What is religion's role in the formation, observance, and enforcement of various rules of morality?" In Shermer's view, religion serves as a social institution that has evolved to become an integral mechanism of human culture, whose purpose is to promote a value system integral to the formation and maintenance of social systems. Religious institutions strive to accomplish this through the creation and promotion of myths, and rules of conduct that encourage altruistic behavior. Religions seek to strengthen social communities by enforcing the rules governing human interactions that promote unanimity, while discouraging selfish and overly competitive behaviors, such as greed and avarice, which create social friction. Prior to the formation of the modern nation-state, religion was the only institution capable of maintaining those belief systems upon which pre-nation-state social communities were founded. One classic example of religion's role in building unanimity within a social community can be seen in the re-creation of the Judaic nation state following the period of the Babylonian exile.

# 6

# The Relevance of Sacred Scripture

**"Revelations of wisdom encapsulated within allegory."**

Both Hebrew and Christian Scriptures are human attempts to chronicle in theological terms humankind's understanding of our relationship with our Creator, our struggle to build and maintain a viable social order, and the reason for our being. Neither is a chronicle written with the purpose of documenting the actions of people and events in an historically correct manner. In fact, allegory was used as a medium to attract readers and to portray the magnificence of the theological messages for which both Hebrew and Christian Scriptures were written.[13] Despite the fact that many fundamentalists base their understanding of the Scriptures' messages on the literal text, any real understanding of any given author's purpose requires study. This is best accomplished via by the reading of a variety of scholastic studies of a particular text, which are available in commentaries written for this purpose. To claim otherwise is ridiculous, because without knowing a particular author's purpose, identifying the intended audience, and gaining an understanding of the historical reality which motivated the author to write the text, it is impossible to gain any reasonable understanding of any particular text's meaning.

In regard to the use of allegory, let us look at 2 Kings, chapter 2, verse 11, as an example of its usage: "As they (Elijah and Elisha) walked on conversing, a flaming chariot and flaming horses came between them, and Elijah went up to heaven in a whirlwind." Now was this event historical, or allegorical? It doesn't take a scholar to figure out that this is an allegorical account of Elijah's death and Elisha's appointment as his successor. But, significantly, Elijah's ascension is one of the very few breaches of the wall of death made by the Hebrew Scriptures, and this account becomes one of the future justifications for belief in the resurrection of Jesus.[14] In this case, since Elijah is described not as dying, but rather as being taken (by YHWH), he need not be subject to being resurrected, but rather as having the capacity to return from his heavenly journey to announce the Messiah's arrival. An anticipation, which is characterized by the gospel writer John (in his chapter 1, verses 19–21) in an encounter between John the Baptist and officials from Jerusalem, when he is asked, "Who are you? Are you Elijah?" It is no coincidence that all the gospel writers (Mark, Matthew, Luke, and John) incorporate John the Baptist's appearance with the beginning of Jesus' ministry. Whether or not stated, it is implied that the Baptist's appearance is likened to Elijah's foretold expected appearance harkening the coming of the Messiah. So, what we encounter in Hebrew Scripture, we repeatedly see again in the Christian Scripture's account of Jesus' life and ministry. This is especially true when Jesus is also later described in Christian Scripture as ascending into heaven, but without the flaming horses and chariot.

The bottom line is that to understand the who, what, where and why of the gospel accounts relating to Jesus, it is necessary to understand the how and why the gospel writers used Hebrew Scripture to define him and his ministry. Jesus was described as having the power to cure the sick, feed the hungry, teach with authority, and go up the mountain to converse with the prophets. In each of these cases, these activities were also attributed to major prophets of antiquity in Hebrew Scripture. This linkage to the prophets was the device by which the gospel writers made Jesus and his ministry understandable to their Jewish readers. In conclusion, my comments on Sacred Scripture were written to encourage thoughtful reflection, rather than to advance any particular interpretation. Most of us, especially in my case, don't have the resources to devote our lives to the scholarly study of Hebrew and Christian Scriptures. Just the language skills involved in any thoughtful critical analysis of scripture is way beyond my capability. If by chance you are confronted by someone who parrots literal quotations of scripture, just remember that what we read in our particular vernacular language (English in my case) had to go through several levels of translation (the use of Hellenistic [Koine] Greek to describe what was spoken in Aramaic, which was then translated into Latin [forth century in the case of the gospels], which then was finally translated into the vernacular of the modern reader). So, beware of nonscholar fundamentalists who lay claim to any great insight based on a literal interpretation of scripture.

# 7

# Jesus

**"A Man whose Ministry's triumph over death gave us the
hope of eternal life."**

Two thousand years ago a man emerged, who so reflected those
qualities we attribute to God (faithfulness, empathy, love, humil-
ity), that we still strive to better know and emulate him. Since
Jesus did not claim any form of divinity, but rather thought of
himself as a prophet (Mark 6:4; Luke 13:33), it is my belief that
in our attempts to understand him, we should judge him and his
ministry as we would the person and works of any other human
being. In fairness to him, we must remember that when he walked
this earth, he was flesh-and-blood just like us. And as a very human man, he laughed and cried, just as we laugh and cry, for all
the same reasons we do. When Jesus defined himself as "Son of
Man," by definition, he was characterizing himself as a "human
one."[15]

Jesus left no written record, so the only means available for
verifying his existence is by the effect he had on the people who
encountered him. Those who were drawn to him and his teachings
told others and from these conversations an oral tradition was carried forth to the succeeding generation chronicling him and his
teachings. At a point in time, about thirty to forty years following
his death, Paul and Mark took up the pen and used the stories
outlined in oral tradition, and perhaps even some written sources

to describe who Jesus was and the importance of his ministry and teachings to a wider Greek-speaking audience. Later, the evangelists Luke, Matthew, and John would, through their genius, further develop Paul's and Mark's understanding of how Jesus reflected God's presence in the here-and-now of the physical world. All four evangelists (Mark, Luke, Matthew and John), each following his particular theological interest, accomplished this through the use of pronouncement stories, miracle stories, parables, and aphorisms—methods of communication which were quite familiar to their Jewish readers, because they followed the traditions of those writers who wrote Hebrew Scripture.

Jesus' public teaching started following the execution of John the Baptist. Up to that time his ministry had paralleled the Baptist's. It is probable that Jesus could even have been a disciple of John. Both baptized those who sought them out on the banks of the River Jordan. Following the Baptist's arrest, Jesus stopped baptizing and sought out people in their synagogues and in the countryside of Galilee rather than waiting for them to seek him out. He may have done this to avoid arrest by King Herod Antipas.

Jesus' message was that the coming of the Kingdom was imminent, meaning that God was coming in, with power and strength, to defeat the powers of evil and usher in the inauguration of the salvation of Israel. By proclaiming this message, Jesus was repeating the prophesies of Isaiah, where the coming of the reign of God is a central theme.[16] Nothing I have ever read suggests that Jesus' purpose was directed toward the establishment of a new religion. Rather, his intent was to outline a new understanding among his fellow Jews as to how they could prepare themselves for the coming of God's kingdom.

What made Jesus different from other teachers of his time was that he taught that God's demands were not limited to just outward conformity to the law, but applied to the whole person, and not to just love of a neighbor, but to love of an enemy (Matt. 5:21–48). For Jesus, God's demands were summed up in this double commandment of love, rather than any form of ritual or rote observance of religious law. At the personal level, it is obvious that Jesus felt great empathy for the people he encountered, many of whom were excluded from full participation in the Jewish social order because of a physical defect or disease. In many of the accounts of Jesus' ministry, he was described as being moved, out of pity, to restore those who had suffered some form of estrangement to reacceptance by the communities in which they lived. In contrast, the religious leaders of his time were more interested in protecting the existing political/religious social order, from which they derived their social position and livelihood.

The Jerusalem of Jesus' time was a city governed by a Roman governor and occupied by a Roman military force. To the extent possible, it was Roman policy to use indigenous members of occupied territories to govern the day-to-day activities of any given populace. That is, as long as those indigenous leaders did what the Romans wanted them to do. So it was that the religious authorities in Jerusalem, at the time of Jesus' last visit, had a vested interest in suppressing any fellow Jew whose activities threatened to upset the delicate balance that existed between them and their Roman overlords. This was especially true during Passover celebrations when Jerusalem's population was increased by thousands of Jewish pilgrims, who for the most part hated their Roman occupiers. As a consequence, the Romans brought in additional military forces and maintained a high state of military readiness during Passover celebrations. For Jesus and those who followed him into Jerusalem, this was the "perfect storm," as Jesus' presence in Jerusalem would have quickly become known to the city's Jewish religious authorities. The messianic enthusiasm that he evoked among the crowds within the city would have been seen as a threat to the public order, which would have had the potential of provoking Roman military intervention. Any provocation of this magnitude would have indeed destroyed the delicate balance of power that existed between the Jewish leadership and Roman authorities. To preserve their positions of power, the Jewish leaders eliminated the threat posed by Jesus by arresting him on the claim that he was a messianic pretender. It was on this basis that he was put to death by crucifixion.

By killing Jesus, the religious authorities of Jerusalem eliminated a Jewish reformer, maintained the status quo, and gave rise to the eventual establishment of a new religion, called Christianity—a religious sect built upon the fact that Jesus and his teachings could not be suppressed by his death. Death could not restrain Jesus, because those who followed him recognized that he spoke and acted on behalf of God, rather than himself. This is why the religious authorities who sought to suppress his teachings by killing him failed. By killing Jesus, they actually brought about his physical resurrection within those who loved and carried his teachings to each succeeding generation. In essence, his death—a singular event—empowered the plurality of Jesus' physical resurrection. A recurring physical resurrection called forth by those of faith, gathering in his name, through baptism, by prayer, and through the celebration of the Holy Eucharist. Faith is the key to understanding the concept of Jesus' resurrection. This is clearly exemplified in Luke's account of "The Appearance on the Road to Emmaus"(Luke 24:13–31), "when the two travelers' eyes were opened and they recognized him." For those two travelers, Jesus was physically resurrected in the person of the fellow traveler that they had befriended. As in the case of the two travelers, we too can witness Jesus' resurrection. All we have to do is open our "eyes" to his presence within whatever form he manifests himself.

# 8

# From Jewish Sect to Christianity

### "Christianity the unforeseen Consequence of war"

It is no accident that Jesus and his disciples are portrayed by the writers of the gospels as coming to the Temple to worship. At the minimum, Jesus, with his family, or later his disciples, most likely visited Jerusalem at least once a year, as part of the annual Passover observance. Hints of Jesus' familiarity with Jerusalem, and the Temple are revealed in Mark's, Matthew's and Luke's (Mark 11: 1–3,Matt. 26:18–19, and Luke 19:30–31) gospel descriptions of Jesus' Passover entrance into Jerusalem. It is information such as this that clearly portrays Jesus and his disciples as Aramaic-speaking, observant Jews, whose sole purpose was to seek the reformation of Judaism. It is within this context that his disciples saw him as the promised Messiah—the Messiah being the longed-for, "Lord's anointed" (1 Sam. 2:10, 12:3; 2 Sam 23:1; etc.), whose reign would be characterized by everlasting earthly justice, security, and peace.[17] Since Jesus' death is set by most authorities as having occurred during the year 30 C.E., how is it that about forty years later, approximately during the year 70 C.E., Jesus' Judaic reformation movement is found to have metamorphosed into a community distinct from Israel, with its own creed and cult?[18] A community whose followers were called "Christians" by both friend and foe. This community of Christians, being now comprised of both Jewish and Gentile members, who believed that

Jesus was the Messiah, but whose Jewish followers, unlike those of a generation ago, found themselves estranged from Judaism. Antioch in Syria was the locale in which this community was centered—Antioch being a refuge for Christians of Jewish heritage, who had fled Jerusalem.[19] Could it be that those events in Jerusalem that prompted this community to abandon their homes, and seek refuge in areas such as Antioch, underlay the causation for the development of the non-Judaic sect we call Christianity?

In his book, *Christianity: Essence, History, and Future,* Hans Kung tells us that following Jesus' crucifixion in the year 30 C.E., up to 62 C.E., Jerusalem remained the center of the Jesus messianic movement, especially for Jewish followers. Peter was the initial spokesman for "The Twelve," with James and John also having a lot of influence over the community of followers. Paul at this time was establishing communities of believers (both Jewish and Gentile) in areas which we now know as Greece, Macedonia, and Turkey. Paul, with Peter's support, began reaching out to Gentiles, and with James's eventual consent, these new converts were exempted from the strict observance of Judaic Law (especially as it applied to dietary requirements and circumcision), thereby broadening the appeal of Gentile conversion. With Peter leaving Jerusalem sometime within this period, perhaps to journey to Rome, James became the leader of the predominantly Jewish messianic community in Jerusalem. As leader of this predominantly Jewish community of believers, James remained an advocate of the strict observance of Judaic Law for those within this locale. This formation of two distinct groups within Jesus' messianic community raised tensions within at least one community of Jewish followers. This tension manifested itself specifically in Galatia's Jewish messianic community, as they protested against the exemptions granted Gentiles. They advocated that all Gentile converts be subject to the full observance of the Law. This issue was not resolved until it was submitted to the Apostolic Council in Jerusalem in the year 48 C.E. The bottom line in all this is that Jerusalem obviously was still the center of the Jewish messianic movement up to this period of time, which means that they were being tolerated up to this point by both the Romans and the Sadducean leadership. So, what happened to change this?

According to the Jewish historian Josephus, James (described as the brother of Jesus) and a number of other Jewish Christians were condemned to death by the Jewish court in Jerusalem (the Sanhedrin) in or about the year 62 C.E.[20] It is believed that those condemned were charged with "transgression of the Law." It is interesting to note that the Pharisees in Jerusalem, who were committed to the strict observance of Judaic Law, protested against this act of judicial murder by the Jewish leadership.[21] Hans Kung suggests that James and the messianic movement he led were viewed as a threat to the political order of Jerusalem. Paul was also arrested during this period of time and, following a two-year trial in Caesarea, was executed in Rome in 64 C.E. Paul, being a Roman citizen, had a claim to legal rights, which postponed the judgment against him. James and the others murdered in Jerusalem, not being citizens in Rome, had no right of appeal to the emperor, as did Paul.

In the year 66 C.E. the Zealots, a coalition of anti-Roman Jewish revolutionaries, rose up in rebellion against the Roman occupation of Judea, and successfully defeated the Roman Jerusalem garrison. Fighting between Roman military forces and Jewish revolutionary forces also extended to other locales in Judea, with varying degrees of success for the Zealots. The death of the Roman Emperor Nero during this period distracted Roman military commanders, as they positioned themselves for possible succession to the position of emperor. As a consequence, the Roman military commander in Judea fought a holding action until such time as the new emperor assumed control of the government. Once this was settled, Rome deployed sufficient military forces to overwhelm the Zealots. In the course of defeating their enemies, the Romans destroyed the city of Jerusalem. The Temple, in particular, was looted and destroyed. I believe that it is safe to assume that prior to the actual beginning of the revolt against the Romans, the political environment in Jerusalem must have been very tense. The Jewish ruling classes within Jerusalem, especially the Sadducees, had the most to lose if they fell out of favor with the Romans. So they must have been very suspicious of any group, or individual, whose actions or presence had the potential to threaten their interests. This was most likely their motivation for their persecution of those identified as members of the Jewish messianic community. This would account for their murdering James, Stephen, and others by stoning, and demanding the Roman execution of Paul. The fact that the Pharisees, who advocated strict observance of the Law, objected to the execution of James and other members of the Jerusalem group points to the falseness of the Sanhedrin's actions.[22] These tensions and murderous acts of self-preservation by the ruling classes of Jerusalem most likely prompted anyone having any issue with them to flee the city. Once the Zealots assumed control of the city, they in turn murdered anyone who opposed them, further motivating many residents to flee. Since the Zealots considered the Sadducees as Roman collaborators, they were in turn murdered and they disappeared from the pages of history.

Up to the destruction of Jerusalem and the Temple in 70 C.E., both non-messianic Jews and messianic followers of Jesus were held together by communal worship in the Temple. Loss of the Temple and the priests who governed those worship rituals within it broke this bond of common worship. Under the leadership of the Pharisees, Judaism redefined itself and assumed a synagogue-oriented form of worship. In this new setting of decentralized congregational worship, adherence to the Torah ("the Law") became an even more important element of Jewish worship. The beliefs of the messianic Jews, and especially those uncircumcised Gentile followers of Jesus' messianic sect, became more and more problematic for Jews. This eventually led to the excommunication of those followers of Jesus' messianic sect. This separation of the two groups lead to the eventual development of modern Judaism and Christianity. Over time, Jesus' messianic movement gave up its attempt to convince Jews that Jesus was the Messiah and directed its conversion efforts toward Gentile pagans. From this estrangement was born Christianity, in large part an unforeseen consequence of war.

# 9

# Early Faith Disputes

**"Issues between orthodoxy and heresy have more often than not been decided by 'Force of Arms and Happenstance' rather than on the merits of theology,"**

Although Jesus was an observant, devout Jew, his understanding of how Judaism should be practiced differed dramatically from those who defined its orthodoxy, the Sadducees, the Scribes, and to a lesser extent, the Pharisees. They viewed Jesus as a blasphemous heretic, and rather than debate their differences, they engineered his murder, which seemed to be the norm for reconciling religious doctrinal differences during this period of time. This being a product of the fact that control of religious practice was an integral component of the exercise of political power. Unfortunately for us, this marriage of religion and politics is still used by a variety of groups within our time to maintain positions of power. And, as in the case of Jesus, murder still seems to be a favorite means of limiting dissent.

It is to the credit of the followers of Jesus that when they were confronted with the first major post-crucifixion issue, as to whether Gentile converts had to submit to Judaic Law (especially circumcision and dietary constraints) Paul, Peter, James, and the others comprising the first Apostolic Council, reached an agreement following a thorough discussion of the issue. The importance of their decision to exempt Gentiles from the strict observance of Judaic Law should never be minimized, because it opened up Christianity to the whole world and ensured its survival. In the absence of this reaching out to Gentiles, and the acceptance of parallel communities of faith (Jewish and Gentile), Christianity would most likely have "died on the vine," following destruction of Jerusalem, the Temple, and the reorganization of Judaism into a synagogue-based form of worship. This die-off did occur within Jewish Christian communities following their excommunication from synagogue worship. Having lost the ability to practice the tenets of early Christianity within the context of their Jewish traditions, they either had to renounce Christian practices to retain access to Jewish religious institutions and communities, or join the newly emerging Greek-speaking Gentile Christian community to remain faithful to Christian practices. One can only imagine how traumatic this estrangement for Jewish Christians would have been. It is logical to assume that for most Jewish Christians caught up in this dilemma, they chose to recant their beliefs in Jesus to avoid excommunication. This thesis would help explain why the rapid growth of Christianity occurred within the Greek-speaking Gentile world, while at the same time, Jewish Christian communities diminished over time. As previously stated, the pressure on Jewish followers of Jesus to re-embrace Judaic orthodoxy must have been tremendous. Few would have found it easy to assimilate into Greek-speaking communities, as differences in language and custom would have presented significant barriers. Those Jewish Christians who could do neither must have ended up in a never-never land of isolated sects of belief.

The decline of the Jewish Christian community had a profound effect on how Jesus and his ministry were to be understood. Jewish Christians viewed Jesus within the context of Jewish history. To Jewish Christians, Jesus was God's "anointed." It was his purpose to declare that God's Kingdom was at hand, and that he was God's messenger. They did not consider him as God in human form. This is why Jewish followers of Jesus were able to claim fidelity to Judaism and worship in the Temple up to the time of the Zealot's revolt against the Roman occupation of Judea. On the other hand, the Gentile Greek-speaking followers of Jesus were not under the constraints of Jewish tradition. They were far more influenced by Hellenistic concepts of divinity. So, as the Jewish Christian community declined, so did their influence diminish as to how Jesus and his ministry were to be understood. Conversely, as the Gentile Christian community assumed dominance over Christianity, so did its Hellenistic philosophical beliefs gain dominance over the evolution of Christian theology. This process of the establishment of Christian orthodoxy came to a head during the fourth century, when the Emperor Constantine called the bishops of the empire together in Nicaea. He ordered this council to define Christian orthodoxy in order to avoid political instability within the Roman Empire arising out of ill-defined religious beliefs that invited heresy. Constantine sought political stability through a religious understanding that there was one god, one emperor, one kingdom, one church, and one faith. Constantine achieved his purpose through the exercise of his power as emperor. So it was through the use of government power and happenstance that the Hellenistic paradigm of Christianity triumphed over the Jewish understanding of Jesus and his ministry. So, over time, Jesus grew to be understood as God in human form, rather than as a prophet, remaking a Jewish heresy into Christian orthodoxy.

# 10

# The Role of Women in the Early Church

**"What happened to diminish the role of women in the Christian faith tradition?"**

I can remember the time, during the late 1940s and the 1950s, when women attending Catholic church services were expected to wear some form of head covering and clothe themselves very conservatively. As a young person, I accepted this expectation of the church as an accepted norm, and never questioned it. Now as I look back at that time, I am much more aware of what this expectation signified. I now realize that this practice was motivated by the same male perceptions of women that we now decry in Islamic countries that regulate the conduct of women, even to the point of dictating how they should dress in public.

The fact of the matter is that we humans, at the core of our being, are sexual animals. While our cognitive skills have elevated us to the top of the "food chain," our behavior is often influenced by sexual impulses that mirror our evolutionary past. Attempts to satisfy, or to repress, our sexual impulses can put us in conflict either with others, or with ourselves. Our expressions of sexuality are so fundamental to our human nature that as we formed into social groups, norms were established to regulate their expression. For without regulation, the social order, essential for human survival, could not be maintained. To enforce these norms, severe sanctions against transgressors were applied. As this process evolved over time, religious beliefs became one of the most important societal instruments in the regulation of sexual behavior.

Karen Armstrong, in her book *The History of God* states that in primitive societies women were sometimes held in higher esteem than men. This was especially true in those societies where religious practices reflected the veneration of the female (fertility, etc.). However, Armstrong adds that with the rise of the cities, as masculine qualities of martial physical strength became more valued over female characteristics, women became more marginalized. This was especially true in Greece, where the democratic ideal did not extend to the women of Athens, who lived in seclusion and were despised as inferior beings.[23] Armstrong also tells us that in early Israelite society, women were seen as forceful and equals of their husbands. Some, like Deborah, led armies into battle.[24] However, over time, as Yahweh was seen to have successfully vanquished the other gods and goddesses and became the only god, their religious practices became more male centered and managed by men. While their monotheistic belief stressed that God transcended gender, Yahweh was essentially seen as male. This shift of understanding was accompanied over time by a decline in the status of women within that society.

Based on what the gospels tell us, women played a major role in the ministry of Jesus. He is described as being very comfortable in their presence, even to the point of chastising his apostles for questioning their presence or interaction with him. This high regard for women is especially evident in John's account of Jesus' encounter with the Samaritan woman at the well (John chapter 4). As far as Jewish law and custom were concerned, this encounter was taboo. In the first instance, as a Jew, Jesus was required to avoid all contact with Samaritans of either sex, as they were considered to be ritually impure. In addition to that, encounters between men and women in instances such as that described by John were also taboo. The very fact that the woman was at the well alone, and at a time of day after the women of her village would have normally drawn water as a group, indicates that she was estranged from the other women of her village. This in and of itself was another "red flag" pointing to a problem or irregularity. Additionally, Jesus requested the woman to draw him some water from the well, despite the fact that the Jewish Law forbade him from drinking from any vessel that had been handled by any Samaritan. Not only did Jesus break this taboo, but he then engaged this woman in a conversation, which led her to rush into her village to tell everyone of her encounter with him. By this woman's willingness to share her encounter with Jesus with her fellow villagers, she was elevated to the status of a disciple in the eyes of her community.

However, as Huns Kung, in his book, *The Catholic Church,* tells us, the establishment of church hierarchical structures in the fourth century was accompanied by a hostility to sexuality.[25] This followed the increase in male domination, especially in the sphere of the sacral. Countless theologians and bishops advocated the inferiority of the females. Even Clement of Alexandria (150–215 C.E.) argued for the subordination of women to men.[26] The letters of St. Jerome (347–420 C.E.) teem with loathing of the female, to the point of sounding deranged.[27] Tertullian, an early church theologian (160–220 C.E.), castigated women as evil temptresses, while St. Augustine (354–430 C.E.) was puzzled that God should have made the female sex after all, since Adam could have better enjoyed the friendship of other men. In his opinion, a woman's only function was childbearing, which unfortunately passed the contagion of Original Sin to the next generation, like a venereal disease.[28]

It doesn't take a genius to see what was happening between the time of Jesus' ministry and the development of a male-led religious hierarchical institution. In the world of the male religious mind, women were viewed as a distraction, perhaps even as a threat. The very sight of women threatened to bring to mind that which was earthly and sinful. Oh how simple it could be if they weren't around to invade the male religious mind with thoughts of sex. Could it be that the true source of Christianity's male-driven hostility toward women springs from mind-sets that have been interrupted by ruminations triggered by the sight or thought of an attractive woman? Ruminations that conjure up feelings of guilt for having allowed the sanctity of the mind to be transgressed by worldly passions. Might those men, who had faced this dilemma, have prayed "Lord, if only you could free me of those distractions by which Satan seeks to excite my earthly passions, might I better achieve that which is truly sublime." In other words: "No girls allowed!"

# 11

# The Issue of Jesus' Nature

**"Who really decided how Jesus was related to God?"**

As stated earlier in this text, when Peter, Paul, and James and other members of the Apostolic Council met in Jerusalem in 48 C.E. and decided to exempt Gentiles from the requirements of Judaic Law, they set the stage for the eventual clash between the Hellenistic and Judaic understandings of Jesus' relationship with God the Father. This issue lay dormant until Christians were freed from the threat of persecution in 313 C.E. It was finally realized by the emperor Galerius, before his death in 311 C.E, that the empire's attempts to exterminate Christianity had failed, including the last great persecution led by the previous emperor, Diocletian. Galerius' successor was Constantine. While no Christian, Constantine was a smart, hard man of power. It was he, with his coregent of the Eastern Empire, Licinius, who in 313 C.E. promulgated the Constitution of Milan that granted unlimited freedom of religion to the whole empire.[29]

Constantine was neither a pious Christian nor a hypocrite. Rather, he was an astute statesman who coolly took Christianity into the calculations of his power politics, which he knew were not free from superstition. In 324 C.E., he defeated Licinius, his coemperor, who practiced paganism, to become the sole ruler of the empire. Upon consolidating power, Constantine then decreed the empire-wide toleration of a wide variety of religious cults. As a part of his religious reforms, Constantine also abolished crucifixion, introduced Sunday as a day of legal festival, and permitted the Christian church to receive legacies. Constantine did all this for very pragmatic reasons. He saw Christianity as an emerging force that could serve to unify the different peoples of the empire around one centralized political base of power. The emergence of Christianity as a state sponsored religion offered him the opportunity to fulfill the empire's need for a philosophical base to support his kingship. To this end, he took measures to ensure that Christianity provided the empire's citizens with a uniform ecumenical creed that supported his concept of: "one god, one emperor, one kingdom, one church, and one faith."[30]

According to Karen Armstrong in her book *A History of God*, a religious doctrinal controversy arose, which threatened Constantine's desire for a uniform ecumenical creed within the Christian Church in or about the year 320 C.E. The controversy was kindled by a charismatic presbyter of Alexandria, named Arius, who challenged his bishop to explain how Jesus Christ could have been God in the same way as God the Father. While not denying the divinity of Christ, Arius argued that it was blasphemous to think the he was divine by nature, since Jesus himself was quoted as saying that the Father was greater than he was. His bishop, Alexander of Alexandria, realizing that Arius was raising a vital question relating to the very nature of God, quickly counterargued that the Creator, God the Father, and the Redeemer, Jesus Christ, were one. Both parties took their arguments to the streets, and soon the members of the laity were debating the issue as passionately as the presbyter and bishop. The controversy became so heated that the emperor Constantine himself intervened and summoned a synod to meet in Nicaea (within modern Turkey) to settle this issue. Up to this point in church history, there was no official orthodox position to give guidance as to who was right or wrong, although Arius's name later became a byword for heresy.[31]

When the bishops gathered at Nicaea (May 20, 325 C.E.), Alexander's brilliant assistant, Athanasius, took the lead in defending his theological position. Although very few of the attending bishops shared Athanasius's view of Christ's nature at the onset of the synod, he was able to impose his theology on the delegates, for few could withstand the empirical pressure applied to gain their support of the creed Constantine wanted them to adopt.

Upon the delegates' approval of the Nicaea Creed, it became the official Christian doctrine that Creator and Redeemer were one. It is interesting to note that even with the adoption of the creed, this dispute within the church continued for another sixty years, eventually giving rise to the concept of the Trinity—a doctrine that was a far cry from how the early Jewish disciples of Jesus would have defined his relationship with God the Father.

# 12

# The Relevance of Faith

**"Faith allows us to acknowledge the dangers and uncertainties of life, while empowering us to strive for its joyful fulfillment."**

As I look back to my childhood, I remember finding a great sense of peace in the fact that I had a strong sense of being part of a large extended family, which had a close relationship with the Catholic Church. Never for a moment did I have any doubt as to who I was, how I related to others, and what my place in the universe was. Family and Church were institutions that were at my disposal should I need support in dealing with any form of adversity. All I had to do was ask for help, or use the insight of family and religious values to guide me through any challenge confronting me. On many hot summer days during my youth I found comfort, and refuge, in the cool interior of my parish church. For me, my parish church represented the ultimate "safe haven," or "sanctuary," a memory I carried into adulthood. I am not saying that I became a very pious person, but rather that I became so grounded in my faith tradition that it became a great resource for me during my military service, my law-enforcement career, marriage, parenthood, and senior years.

In his book *Does God Exist?* Hans Kung describes a concept called "fundamental trust," which, I believe, shares many of the attributes which are linked to the concept of faith—faith being defined as: *"Trust, confidence, complete acceptance of a truth which cannot be demonstrated or proved by the process of logical thought."*[32]

While Kung distinguishes between the two concepts and does not link them together, he does indicate that others do see the two being related to one another. He defines "fundamental trust" as follows:

> Fundamental trust means that a person, in principle, says "Yes" to the uncertain reality of himself and the world, making himself open to reality and able to maintain this attitude consistently in practice. This positive fundamental attitude implies an antinihilistic fundamental certainty in regard to all human experience and behavior, despite persistent, menacing uncertainty.[33]

Both these concepts share at least one particular component. Each is based upon the possession of a particular attitude that reflects a belief that the glass is half full. This is an attitude formed upon the foundation of human experience through time. We could call it acquired "wisdom," which has as its foundation all the prior experiences of humankind. This acquired wisdom rejects the nihilistic belief that we die into oblivion. As in fundamental trust, it acknowledges the uncertainties of reality, accepts them, and marches on in daily life with head held high, rather than yielding to the darkness of nihilism. A religious faith based in reality can in particular be the doorway to a future reality grounded in mutual respect, a sense of self-worth, fulfillment, and hope. Yes, while we might be likened to fleas on an elephant (our physical reality), we rejoice for having the opportunity to share this journey through time and space.

# 13

# Other Religions and Faith Traditions

**"Let us never be so ignorant, or arrogant that we fail to honor all teachings which through time have striven to elevate humankind's attentiveness toward the needs of others."**

By and large, most of us are born into the particular religious faith tradition that we practice, and take for granted that our affiliation is superior to others. In those instances where we, as adults, actually selected our religious affiliation, this feeling of superiority may even be more pronounced, even though it has been my observation that social/emotional factors, rather than knowledge of a sect's theology, are the primary motivation leading to a conversion. Unfortunately, in both instances, I find that both categories of adherents lack what I would consider to be an adult level of understanding of the history and belief tenets of their affiliation. Yet this lack of knowledge doesn't seem to reduce the assumption that their inherited or selected faith tradition is superior to those practices of other religions. Admittedly, if we didn't have some degree of confidence in the superiority of our faith affiliation, how could we ever feel comfortable with our faith practices? What we must resist is the comfort that a given system of faith practices is superior to our neighbors' faith practices, just because we espouse it. Overconfidence in the superiority of a religious affiliation can easily take the form of a bias that colors our perceptions of other religious affiliations, even though we may be totally ignorant of their faith practices. It is at this level of bias that assumptions of a religious sect's superiority become problematic. Bias born of ignorance increases the probability that an adherent's interactions with people of other faith traditions are going to be fraught with misunderstandings, misunderstandings that can lead to conflict.

In and of itself, if your religious affiliation meets your needs and motivates you to practice the Golden Rule (Confucius, The Doctrine of the Mean, 13, c. 500 B.C.E.: *What you do not want others to do you, do not do to others*, any religious bias that you may harbor is of no great consequence. However, if this is not the case, and your creed's bias is such that you can't honor the faith's traditions (that also adhere to the tenets of the Golden Rule) of others that don't match your creed's, then your affiliation fails the "smell test."

Dysfunctional religious cults that periodically emerge under the leadership of some charismatic leader, that support and encourage sociopathic behavior of their members, do not deserve to be regarded as valid faith traditions. There is something to be said for faith traditions that have withstood the test of time, because over time the common sense of the members has usually moderated the more radical aspects of their belief tenets (such as practices associated with human sacrifice, as alluded to in Genesis, chapter 22). Remember the old saying, "All things in moderation." This adage is especially true when it comes to questions associated with overzealous religious practices. Think of it this way: We are all on a journey ... a journey of life ... and religion is like a system of navigation that serves to assist you in the circumnavigation of your life. How well your faith tradition accomplishes this should be the ultimate test of your religion's relevance. If your current faith tradition doesn't pass this test, then I would strongly suggest that you do your homework, become a knowledgeable student of religion, and seek an affiliation that better helps you to meet the challenges of life. In doing this, you will find that in addition to becoming a much more knowledgeable parishioner, you most likely will find that your religious biases are much diminished too.

While we all harbor some bias favoring a particular thing, or point of view, these inclinations need not be problematic unless they are based upon an emotional, rather than a knowledge-based, response to choice. This is especially true in the case of religious bias, because of the diversity of faith traditions that surround us. Interactions between different faith traditions, characterized by insensitivity and intolerance, born out of a biased view held by at least one of the parties, can quickly undermine the original purpose of the interaction. The potential power of bias to degrade fruitful interactions between different faith traditions, unfortunately, dominates the news of our day.

Religious bias in its extreme forms generates a level of exclusivity found in fundamentalists sects within Judaism, Islamist Islam, and Christianity. Among the traits of exclusivity that these fundamentalist sects share in common, is that each of them claims to have the exclusive view of the "truth," as it relates to our Creator's revelation to humanity. Another trait that these sects share is that they are in rebellion against modernity, as they view science's findings, as it relates to our origins and history, as a threat to their fundamentalist tenets of faith. In their efforts to "turn the clock back" to a time of simplicity, these sects also exhibit traits of political aggressiveness, authoritarianism, and repressive social/political views. Astute readers of the gospels will quickly note that these are the same traits exhibited by those who sought to destroy Jesus' ministry and crucify him.

# 14

# Prayer

**"If you really want to converse with God, speak to your inner self."**

Prayer is a form of communication. It may be the most useful tool that we humans possess to empower those attributes which are unique to our persons. The Catechism of the Catholic Church defines it as follows: "The elevation of the mind and heart to God in praise of his glory; a petition made to God for some desired good, or in thanksgiving for a good received, or in intercession for others before God. Through prayer the Christian experiences a communion with God through Christ in the Church." As you can see, the Catholic Church views prayer as a Christian endeavor based on a recognition that Jesus Christ is its focus. Its Catechism also categorizes prayer as follows: "Vocal, Meditative, and Contemplative." The church even warns its faithful against viewing prayer as a simple psychological or ritualized activity. In other words, prayer must come from the heart and have a focus upon something beyond the physiological.

In light of the fact that I believe that all of humanity has been created in the image of our Creator and that God's Spirit dwells within each of us, I am of the mind that prayer is a resource available to us all, without qualification. I also believe that the focus of prayer should be directed inward toward the center of our being. At the very core of our being, beyond ego and all worldly distractions, resides God's Spirit. It is this residence of God within us that distinguishes us from any other earthly creature. It is also at this point within our being that I believe all those gifts bestowed upon us through time by our Creator reside. Accordingly, our inner-selves could be viewed as a kind of a computer hard-drive from which these unrealized gifts in the form of potentialities can be accessed. Prayer, being the code by which these dormant potentialities can be brought forward into our consciousness.

It is not by self-destructive, mind-altering misbehavior that those hidden attributes that lay at the core of our being can be brought forth into our consciousness. Rather, it is through the deliberate, acutely conscious exploration of the site where God's Spirit resides within us that we are able to gain access to the full range of our potentiality. Prayer, in the form of a conversation with God's Spirit within us, is one of the means by which each of us can embrace the full reality of our gifted nature. Introspective prayer is indeed the catalyst by which each of us can gain access to those qualities of God that reside within us and put them to use. The discovery and liberation of these intrinsic talents can in turn enrich the quality of our lives beyond measurement. However, the achievement of this level of introspective prayer requires a level of honesty that rejects all forms of falsehood and dishonest rationalization. You must seek peace with yourself and others. It is upon this foundation of reality and truth that your conversation with the Spirit that dwells within you can be used to seek out your true potential. A conversation that will transform you beyond all previous expectations, and lead to your liberation from all artificial constraints.

# 15

# The Trinity

**"How did we come up with the idea that our God is part of a three-coequal partnership?"**

During my early elementary school religious studies I struggled to reconcile teachings that taught me that there was but one God, while, at the same time, describing that same one God as being three different, distinct persons. My teacher's response to my dilemma was to tell me that while our belief in a Trinitarian God was an important tenet of Christian doctrine, I should not think too much about it, since I would never be able to understand it. How true those words were, since after sixty years, I still don't understand this tenet of faith, which teaches that three coequal partners exist in one Godhead.

Since I now believe that what we call God exists beyond our physical universe, I also have come to the conclusion that we humans lack any frame of reference by which any such understanding of our God's nature could be gained. So, if God's nature is unknowable, then how did the belief in a Trinitarian (three coequal partners in the Godhead) come to be such an important Christian doctrine? Since Christians have come to worship Jesus as a god (to deify him), could it be that this concept was a device by which the early Christian church could defend itself against charges that it had rejected belief in the monotheistic tradition of the God of Israel? The earliest New Testament (NT) evidence for a tripartite formula comes in 2 Corinthians 13:13, where Paul wishes that the grace of the Lord Jesus, the love of God, and the communion of the Holy Spirit be with the people of Corinth. Otherwise, no other NT writer addresses the issue of a Trinitarian relationship between God, Jesus, and the Holy Spirit.[34] Since no other NT sources speak in support of this concept, it is no wonder that my early religious studies teacher discouraged my further inquiry into the nature of the Trinity.

I do find it interesting, though, that while the early Christian Church rightfully acknowledged the unknowable quality of God's nature, it could turn around during the fourth century and define God's nature as having a Trinitarian quality. Would it not have been better, for the faithful of every succeeding generation, for the church to have admitted that God's nature was beyond their knowing? But then again, the early church would have had a problem justifying the deification of Jesus. I think that the closest we humans can come to an understanding of God's nature is through the study of ourselves and the universe in which we reside. This is why an understanding of Jesus and the historical and religious context from which he came is so important in this endeavor. It is from the thousands of years of humanity's struggle to define the unknowable, by the exemplary lives of individuals such as Jesus, and the study of our universe, that we can piece together a modicum of a frame of reference, from which we can deduce the nature of our Creator. To do otherwise is to engage in pure speculation.

# 16

# The Concept of Evil

**"In the absence of the human capacity to exercise 'free will,' evil cannot exist."**

Evil is defined in *Webster's Encyclopedic Dictionary* as being "what is morally wrong, what hinders the realization of the good." It further defines the word "moral" as "concerned with right and wrong and the distinction between them." *The Catechism of the Catholic Church* defines evil as: "The opposite or absence of good" and as for moral evil, it is said that it, "results from the free choice to sin which angels and men have—sin being defined as "an offense against God as well as a fault against reason, truth, and right conscience, sin being a deliberate thought, word, deed, or omission contrary to the eternal law of God."

The key to understanding the nature of evil is that it is a product of an act that is the result of a free-choice decision. *The Catechism of the Catholic Church* defines freedom and responsibility as follows: "Freedom is the power rooted in reason and will, to act or not to act, to do this or that, and to perform deliberate actions on one's own responsibility." In other words, the excuse "The devil made me do it!" is no defense against being held responsible for your evil acts.

Since I believe the realm of the supernatural to be a human construct, I find it difficult to give any credence to any belief in an angelic world that parallels ours. Therefore, I limit the exercise of free will to humankind. Any concern regarding angels having the capacity to sin is beyond my consideration. Also, since all the other life forms that share this planet with us are driven by instinct and lack the facility of free will, it is my belief that evil is limited to the machinations of humans. I propose that at that point in our evolution where we became truly human, and acquired the understanding of the consequences of our acts, we also acquired the facility to engage in acts, now defined as immoral/evil. So, it is my thesis that in the absence of humanity, immorality/evil cannot exist. As a consequence, I propose that any belief in any evil entity, such as Satan, is pointless.

# 17

# Life after Death

**"If there is life after death, what form will this new reality take?"**

Of all the scholars that I am familiar with, and who have sought to address the issue of life after death, I find Hans Kung's explanation, which he outlines in his book *Does God Exist,* the most understandable. It is Kung's thesis that for Christians, our hope for an existence following our physical death is grounded in our believing that a God resurrected Jesus to demonstrate that neither would we be allowed to die into nothingness.[35] This is not a belief that can be proved empirically, just as the existence of God, or the resurrection of Jesus as cited in the New Testament, can neither be proved nor disproved empirically. The foundation of this belief in life after physical death is built solely upon faith—a belief that as Jesus lives eternally through and with God, the God for whom he stood in life and death, so shall we eventually dwell with him in God.

Both religious believer and atheist face the reality of eventual death. To quote Kung, the atheist sees him/herself dying into nothingness, while the religious believer, on the other hand, sees him/herself dying into that absolute last reality, which we call God. While neither belief can be proved or disproved empirically, it is not unreasonable to be attracted to the belief that we die not into nothingness, but into a loving God—a belief that is grounded in an enlightened trust that we are a valued part of God's creation. In other words, a belief that the glass is half full, not half empty.

Kung theorizes that the new resurrected reality is not a return to life as we know it. Our death is not cancelled, but definitively conquered, while not being a continuation of this (physical) life in space and time. Rather, it means a life that bursts through the dimensions of space and time in God's invisible, imperishable, incomprehensible domain. As he sees it, as for God's heaven, he envisions our going into a reality, not going out. A reality, which, if I am interpreting his vision correctly, is the infinite reality for which we were always intended to enter, in contrast to the finite physical world that is our temporary abode.

The big question for me, is whether or not our new after-death reality includes any level of self-consciousness. After all, is it not this facility that makes us unique and distinguishes each of us from all who came before and all who are yet to be born? Scripture speaks of a bodily resurrection after death, but this is not the facility that makes us unique. The matter that makes up our bodies is nothing more than recycled matter that has its origin in the evolution of our universe and will continue through this recycling process through space and time—its life span being limited to the life span of our physical universe, which is not necessarily eternal/infinite.

The difficulty in attempting to answer this question relating to our after-death reality is our lack of any frame of reference. Without a frame of reference, we can only speculate as to the form, if any, in which our after-death reality would manifest itself. Once again it all boils down to having faith in the concept of a loving God willing to rescue us from nothingness. As for me, I am again betting that the glass is half full.

# 18

# The Veneration of Mary, the Mother of Jesus (Marianism)

### "Is Mary the Mother of God, or the Mother of Christ?"

Christian Scripture tells us that Mary of Nazareth, the wife of Joseph, gave birth to a child named Jesus during the year 4 B.C.E., while in the town of Bethlehem. She is mentioned in the context of the marriage feast at Cana (John 2.1–12), at Jesus' crucifixion (but only by John 19:25–27), and in Acts 1.14, the story of Pentecost. The accounts of Mary's later years, death, and assumption into heaven are found in traditions outside the Bible, some as late as the fourth century C.E. These nonscriptural texts include the writings by some of the early church fathers and in the fifth-century deliberations of the Council of Ephesus, where she was proclaimed Theotokos, "God-bearer."

It is through these and other sources that the powerful cult of Mary had its origin and attracted adherents, especially in the Roman Catholic, Anglo-Catholic, and Orthodox churches. Mary has been revered not only as the Mother of God, but also as a pure ever-virgin woman, the perfect mother, the intercessor between human beings and God, and the one who knows the deepest of human suffering, having witnessed the agonizing and humiliating death of her firstborn son. She has been the object of pilgrimages and visions even to the present day. The "Magnificent," attributed to her by Luke at the time of her visit to Elizabeth (Luke . 1:6–55), has been part of Christian liturgy and music for centuries. Mary has been widely honored and even worshiped as representing inner strength and the exaltation of the oppressed over the oppressor.

Non-Christian sources are instructive in tracing parallels to the cult of Mary. Virgin Birth stories (e.g., Hera, Rhea Sylvia, Brigid) were circulated in other cultures, as were tales of mothers mourning lost and deceased children (e.g., Demeter and Persephone; Isis and Horus). Such parallels show that Mary's cult had roots in the worship of the female deities of the Greco-Roman pantheon, pagan cults ultimately eradicated by Christianity. While Mary, in some ways, represents qualities impossible for human beings, especially for women to emulate—ever-virgin, yet motherly; always gentle and obedient to God's will—her attributes nevertheless represent, for many devotees, important female properties not provided by the traditional all-male Trinity. For many, the adoration of a female figure is a vital psychological supplement to their faith?[36]

Hans Kung, in his book *Christianity,* tells us that the concept of Mary being the "Mother of God" was advocated by Cyril of Alexandria during the session of the Council of Ephesus in the year 431. The fact that this took place within this particular locale had a significant influence on the adoption of this theological position. This city's inhabitants had a tradition of pagan worship that included worship of a female deity named the "Great Mother" (originally the virgin goddess Artemis/Diana). The substitution of Mary for their original pagan goddess was accepted with enthusiasm by this city's converts to Christianity, a factor which was cleverly used by Cyril to manipulate the council's decision to declare that Mary was the Mother of God. Conversely, in the Western Church, this concept was slow to develop. In St. Augustine's writings there are neither hymns nor prayers to Mary, not even any relating to a feast of Mary. It wasn't until the sixth century that forms of Latin and German poetry began to appear, and

Mary's name (Mater Dei) was incorporated into the text of the Mass. By the tenth century, legends began to circulate in relation to Mary's miraculous power of prayer. The climax of the medieval cult of Mary occurred during the eleventh/twelfth century during which the theological New Testament understanding of Mary, as the earthly mother of Jesus, shifted to emphasize Mary's cosmic role as the virgin mother of God and queen of heaven. Whereas earlier church fathers had spoken without hesitation about moral faults in Mary, now a perfect sinlessness concept of Mary was increasingly asserted—indeed, a holiness even before her birth. However, the Catholic Church during this period did not proclaim any new Marian dogmas. It was not until the nineteenth and twentieth centuries that Pius IX and Pius XII elevated teachings related to Mary to the status of dogma. The elevation to dogma of Mary's immaculate conception, and her bodily assumption to heavenly glory by these popes was closely paralleled with proclamations related to the dogma associated with the primacy and infallibility of the popes, and their opposition to modernity.[37]

The question relating to whether Mary should be seen as the Mother of God or as the Mother of Christ, points directly to the more important question of how we should view Jesus. Should we as Christians view Jesus in New Testament terms (as a very human being who, by his actions, exemplified those qualities attributed to God), or should we view Jesus as the fourth century-deified second member of the Trinity. If we choose the NT Christ (as a very human man anointed by God), then we should view Mary as his very mortal mother. If on the other hand, we view Jesus as the deified second person of the Trinity (a divine person who walked the earth), then Mary becomes a cosmic virgin receptacle, whose sole purpose was to deliver the divine personage of Jesus into the physical world.

I personally advocate viewing Mary through the lens of the New Testament. She should be defined as the writers of the NT saw her, as a living, breathing, real person, who shared our human attributes, lived out her life, and died as we will all eventually die. I would credit both her and Joseph as having been very good parents. Why, you might ask? Well, because the fruit of their labors was Jesus Christ. So, obviously both Joseph and Mary did a very good job of raising him. The qualities of love, devotion, fidelity, and empathy for others that he exhibited most likely had their origin in the persons of Joseph and Mary. I specifically believe that it does Mary a disservice to relegate her to the role of a cosmic sacred delivery system. She was more than that, as she was too great of a mother to deserve that degree of depersonalization.

I believe that John's NT writings best describe Mary's role in Jesus' life. Her role is especially well described in his accounting of the "The Wedding at Cana" (John 2. 3–5) when Mary directed Jesus' attention to the lack of wine, and then told the servers: "Do whatever he tells you." In essence, in this gospel reading, Mary is being depicted as one of Jesus' first disciples, and her message, "Do whatever he tells you," is in reality a message that is intended to echo through time to every succeeding generation.

In Jn. 19:25–26, Mary is described as "Standing by the cross of Jesus."

She, in other words, was with him throughout his ministry. John is telling us in essence that Mary represents the essence of fidelity to be modeled by all believers. By John's account, Mary, in her humanity, was far more than some cosmic virgin birth delivery receptacle. She was a real person, who in life exemplified those qualities of virtue to which we aspire.

# Notes

1. Catholic Study Bible: "*New American Bible.* Luke, p. 97.
2. Catholic Study Bible: *New American Bible.* Pentateuch, Reading Guide, p. 47.
3. Michael D. Coogan: *The Oxford Companion to the Bible.* pg. 567.
4. Ibid., p. 338.
5. Ibid., p. 173.
6. Hans Kung: *The Beginning of all Things. Science and Religion.* p. 9.
7. Ibid., p. 11.
8. Conway Morris: *Life's Solutions,* p. 151.
9. The Catholic Study Bible: *New American Bible,* Pentateuch, p. 5.
10. *Catechism of the Catholic church.* articles 396–412.
11. Catholic Study Bible: *New American Bible.* Pentateuch, p. 6.
12. Michael Shermer: *The Science of Good & Evil.* p. 18.
13. Hans Kung: *Christianity.* p. 165.
14. Harold W. Hoehner: *The Oxford Companion to the Bible.* p. 182.
15. Reginald H. Fuller: *The Oxford Companion to the Bible.* p. 360.
16. Ibid.
17. John F.A. Sawyer: *The Oxford Companion to the Bible.* p. 513.
18. Karen Armstrong: *A History of God.* p. 80.
19. Hans Kung: *Christianity.* p. 17.
20. Ibid., pp. 85–87.
21. Ibid.
22. Ibid., p. 86.
23. Karen Armstrong: *A History of God.* p. 50.
24. Ibid.
25. Huns Kung: *The Catholic Church.* p. 28.
26. Hans Kung: *Christianity.* p. 154.
27. Karen Armstrong: *A History of God.* p.124.
28. Ibid., p. 123–124.
29. Hans Kung: *Christianity.* pp. 177–182.
30. Ibid., p. 181.
31. Karen Armstrong: *A History of God.* pp. 110–120.
32. The New Lexicon: *Webster's Encyclopedic Dictionary.*
33. Hans Kung: *Does God Exist?* p. 445.
34. Daniel N. Scowalter: *The Oxford Companion to the Bible.* 782.
35. Hans Kung: *Does God Exist.* pp. 678–680.

36. Valerie Abrahamsen: *The Oxford Companion to the Bible*. p. 499.
37. Hans Kung; *Christianity*. pp. 463–458.

# Suggestions for Further Study

It is my hope that what I have written is of some use to those seek-ing a street-level understanding of the theological points covered within this study. As I stated in the introduction, I make no claim to great theological insight. Rather, my objective is to point you, the reader, to those of great insight whose writings can empower you to reach a new level of theological understanding. To that end, may I refer you to the writings of the following authors that I am familiar with and whose writings are referred to in this study:

Gosta W. Ahilstrom: *The History of Ancient Palestine.*
Karen Armstrong: *The Bible, The Great Transformation, Buddha, In the Beginning, Holy War.*
Karl Barth (translated by Paul M. van Buren): *Karl Barth, God Here and Now.*
John Barton and John Muddiman (eds.): *The Oxford Bible Commentary.*
Raymond Brown: *Response to 101 Questions on the Bible The Critical Meaning of the Bible.*
F.F. Bruce: *The New Testament Documents: Are They Reli-able?*
Craig Blomberg: *The Historical Reliability of the Gospels.*
Averv Dulle: *Models of the Church.*
Timothy Ferris: *The Whole Shebang: A State-of-the-Universe(s) Report.*
Israel Finkelstein and Neil Asher: *The Bible Unearthed.*
Thomas Keating: *Open Mind, Open Heart.*

Hans Kung and Julia Ching: *Christianity and Chinese Religions.*

Hans Kung: *Does God Exist?, Christianity, Essence, History and Future Christianity and World Religions, The Beginning of All Things, The Catholic Church, Great Christian Thinkers.*

Lawrence R. Michaels: *The Gospels in their Original Meaning.*

Simon Conway Morris: *Life's Solutions,*
*(Inevitable Humans in a Lonely Universe).*

Joseph Cardinal Ratzinger (Benedict XVI): *Salt of the Earth, God and the World.*

Michael Shermer: *The Science of Good & Evil:*
*Why People Cheat, Gossip, Care, Share, and Follow the Golden Rule.*

Victor J. Sterger: *Timeless Reality (Symmetry, Simplicity, and Multiple Universes).*

Peter M.J. Stravinskas: *The Catholic Church and the Bible.*